Stay ambitious

Table of Contents

Dedication

I'd like to dedicate this book to all the voiceless people around the world. You all could make a difference like Malala, all that it takes is courage. I'd also like to acknowledge Sariah and Drexler Doherty II. Qweti is a big inspiration in my life, so this one's for you! Finally I dedicate this book to anyone who actually opened the cover.

Thank you

God-

Dr. Bill Hennessey-

Dr. Kathie Hennessey-

Kate Reavey-

My Reservation-

Mr. Nexclayum-

Peninsula College-

Tor Parker-

Poetic Blood Quantum-

Ami-

Master Chief-

Muhammad Ali-

Goku-

My future self will laugh at this, because I will get better and better and better and better and better and better and better and better. First project!

Introduction

I'm from that town if you don't keep your mental astound--
potential will drown--
they say nothing but fiends and dealers running around--
n overdosed bodies constantly being found--
I get along with them both--
maybe I'm the greatest the seed for hope/// I remember we'd fly to
the sky before my wolves got high off that dope//
there was loyal n trust now it's just// burnt up foil n empty bottles to
dust// followed by lust//
slow down or your life is just going to be bars n cuffs// I never picked
up drugs but I have scars from night so rough// Enough is enough…
We are our own reason why life is tough// quit blaming the ones who
gave up and gave in are the ones out there doing the raping// cuz
they just don't give a what?// Any girl out there is just a nut// so think
about n try to help out before you call that little girl a slut// but close
your legs baby girl giving it up ain't going to replace that love that
was stolen//we're constantly killing ourselves and that's the pain that
I'm holding//I am far from perfect, I don't even know what my pur-
pose within this earth is but I know it's not worthless//
I learned a lot of values of which is really important, and nothing is
really important however everyone is//it's still hard for me to get close
to somebody, I could look at someone I love and all I could see is
a dead body// just enjoy it all listen kids never slit your wrists just enjoy
it all// the past don't haunt me no more, I don't get sad and I don't
care no more// you could say that's heartless but you prolly never
walked in such a darkness// I'm far from godly my biological moth-
ers name was angel// she fell from heaven while I was being born//
so hell is the only home my soul was ever sworn// there is no rest in
the land of the torn// so tell me if you're falling in hell's abyss, is there
something that exists to grasp n climb up outta this endless life that
torments// and reach heaven where they say life is timeless// my
only hopes of speaking, is to torch this torturous demon that forbids
me from dreaming// even while I'm smiling my soul is constantly
screamin// I'm going crazy all I seek is peace, but all I see is babies
deceased// minds grow deceived and diseased// never played

no victim never asked please// everything my eyes seen made my mind increase// developed a weapon of deadly thoughts that never seem to release n cease the squeeze// how can lies come up out my teeth, when I stand for those struggling just to be able to breath// suffocatin, just waitin, hoping for the day they soul gets to leave// feeling of no escapement// learn patience it'll bring amazement// but with opportunity never offer no hesitation// don't show demonstration of frustration no matter the occasion// always carry confidence burry fear// will yourself through any hell there's a reason why we are all here//
never accept defeat you gotta take your dream and make that your heart beat

Trail of Tears

Dear fry-bread,

  why do we love you when you want us all dead?

Dear fry-bread,

  why do we love you when you want us all dead?

They took all our natural foods

gave us back crumbs

n told us they're feeding us--

So we should be thankful--

That's my short poem.

I hope you understand the history I'm showing.

Dear fry-bread,

  why do we love you, when you want us all dead??

Dear fry-bread,

  why do we love you, when you want us all dead??

Confined

What if we dreamed under the stars?
Sure, physically every moment we breathe
we`re underneath--
But, there`s this ceiling in-between,
this ceiling in-between confines a limit to my dreams--
I often wonder what if these
ceilings have us like flower seeds under a rock--
only some consumes--
in our sense, see in the dark//
most is waiting for a spark--
why do we allow ourselves to forbid us from growing--
I know, I gotta see the beauty that's there--
it has to be-
God loves us this town didn`t survive magically--
but naturally our perspectives of not knowing what divine truth
is,
 leaves us reckless, respect this, hate that, do this despise
that--
....that`s what
is taught.....
I wonder where I would be if I dreamt under stars--
and,
didn`t have this ceiling to confine me--
Oh well, time is borrowed--
I don`t have enough to wait and see...
Smile at the possibility, cry at what`s logically

so to speak--

but ceilings have a peak--

that's what is built

 around us,

I'm going to tear that down--

because I have a belief, that is so strong that nothing could

confine this dream—

Carving Mountains

The blind responds angrily when you learn to see--
they'll tell lies about everything in which you believe--
trying to convince you to leave--
dying to deceive--
they living just to breathe-
I'm existing, to spark change--
light the dark so future life don't look strange--
it's true lost souls are envious of happiness--
they wanna see you suffer--
can't find it on their own so, they place fault on another--
Little did they know is I'm a fighter--
however I tell them I forgive them--
teach them how to live then--
rip the devil beneath their skin--
now they're living //
Live a life worth remembering--
I feel my mind sits seas apart from most human thought--
My spirit is far bigger --
so I let my flame flicker--
trust, no tornadoes or gusts
can wind enough
to douse me out --
I breathe for the betterment of human kind--
no diamond can cut my mind--
You could carve your name with diamonds in mountains--
still, eventually the waves will wash em away like drawing in the

sand--

I use to fear death now I am daring death--

the true and living do not die--

I believe in the sky --

Built to fight, for real can't see how people can stand by while

we just die unnecessarily--

then we raise another generation emotionless because they

are hurt by the world.--

nah not me, I am not owed anything --

my freedom is watching our children dance while I sing--

now that's beautiful, now that's peaceful.--

May not be impressive to an educated man--

still....

I feel wiser than an educated man--

N I am humbled and blessed; knowing they will never under-

stand why I stand--

So I carve in the sand--

watch waves fade it away--

I am not worried that,

the world will forget my name--

In the sky I will stay, I am happy that way--

Hundred Years

Can you tell me what an education is?/
when I'm in these classes that's making a mockery of my culture
devaluing everything I'm fighting to hold on to/
the hypocrisy bothers me//
remember 9/11-
but when I speak on my relatives in mass grave sites, I get re-
sponses life "pfft get over it"//
like the indigenous don't exist anymore, genocide babies got
their mind twisted for gore//
That's why I say, "we're only free if we're willing to be a slave."
However I'm not willing, and I'm still free/
I guess it's a mentality
I excelled the reality set out for me/
no expectations turned into greatness,
and that's to all of the nations/

We survived being on the being on the brink of extinction!!
I'ma let that sink in…

ON the brink of extinction, we'll never stop breathing!!
I'ma let that sink in…

On the brink of extinction, drums and hearts still beating!!
I'ma let that sink in…

Brink of extinction thrown into an abyss without sinking!!
I'ma let that sink in…

They tell us to get over it, when we're still tryna swim to shore
we are now at war trying to save our own souls.
Genocide is on us, and I trust we'll make it back to land//

Because,

over a 100 years of boarding school we still stand!
telling me not to speak my language/well we're still speaking
telling me don't sing my songs/ well we're still singing
telling me it's illegal to dance/ well we're still moving
over a hundred years classified as
heathens
savages
injhuns
reddevils
redskins
uncivilized//
and we are still together.
We will be forever
a hundred years of shaming us
" A good Indian, is a dead Indian"
"Kill the Indian, save the man"
yet, we are still proud--
I'm still loud--

We must save ourselves, it's hard to ask for help--

we'll be misunderstood--

Everything about my culture is beautiful--

how long will it be here?

Remember our values,

don't let who we are pass away with our elders--

I love every song, dance, word, beads, shells, drums, spears,

cedar hats, I love the canoe

love the paddles, love the Snipe and the rattles.

A lot more than physical

we are a band of brothers/

hundred years of tears

and we're still here for each other/

Deny cultural genocide

Rise above it!

You have to love it!

Rise above it!

You have to love it!

Rise above it!

What to live for?

Do you believe your beliefs?

I drop jewels in the gutter/

somewhere in history humans were deceived to misery/

fooling you and me,

that it's material over soul./

Gold over hope/

sell dope for a rope that don't erode/

but, what about your morality?

it's sad to see people buried for some-THING that's pretty but,

petty/

I guess I don't know what the fuck I'm talking about, and that's

a sad reality…

The Eyes of my Enemy

Staring at the eyes of my enemy, I see me--

Staring in the eyes of my enemy, we have the same valor

however we fight for a different creed--

Staring at the eyes of my enemy I feel the spirit and pride of

nationality, same as me--

Staring at the eyes of enemy, I know you're just a man making

a stand--

Staring at the eyes of my enemy I understand his bravery,

protecting his land--

Protecting his pride--

Staring at the eyes of my enemy kills me inside--

Staring at the eyes of my enemy, I salute you man to man--

Staring at the eyes my enemy as he takes his last breath in my

hands--

Fighting you was an honor, there's so much cowards in this

war--

every century there's gore

some people let their life slip away--

Staring at the eyes of my enemy is a reminder of what to fight

for--

warriors don't die easy there's gonna be hell to pay--

Dying free is better than allowing atrocity--

Staring at the eyes of enemy, still full of soul even after his

death--

I hope to shake your hand at the gates--

Be a man take a stand, control your own fate--

don't be a victim to those whom dictate--
nobody is right in any fight
but to be in the fight is right--

Loyalty--
Honor--
Morality--
will not be phased by nobody, handle your responsibilities,
believe your beliefs--
only cowards cover who they truly are--
Honesty is majestic, you better protect it--
No matter the rivalry
live by The Code of Chivalry...

Vagabond

How long must our souls roam

in a mode of a vagabond--

Lost n scared staggering on--

torn from homes--

torn from hope--

torn from meaning--

Scaling a slope

while vultures crow--

dark alleys--

deep valleys--

sharp cuts--

sharp tongues--

stalk rum

stock some,

the barrel's gone--

a grain of faith

a drop of water, in a sand storm--

engaged to alter change,

at the altar engaged, spare change?--

mind weapon, Thought Cannon,

canning canons, elevated canyons--

of course, coarse corpse differ courses--

our knight, hours nights

with no grate, know greats--

 aero arrows, that affect effect--

I'll aisle ail ale addicts--

sent ascent sense, assent your allowed--

speak aloud, it's not odd to be in awed--

Ceilings are sealing, break free--

wild one can't brake me--

my mind is war--

dual duels--

roles rule --

but what's a farrow to a pharaoh?

Eagle amongst seagulls so I stand alone--

feeble fleas flee away from me--

my only weakness is my heroine she's my heroin

that's addiction…

Do you have a headache yet?

Nothing could kill me, only love--

My minds different, either I'm going to change the world or the
world is going to change me

So before I hear em get caught, I may have to kill my dreams
and bury the corpse///

Untitled

All the gold under the moon
wouldn't compare to being next to her--
locked in from the first moment, let the sentence last a while--
her presence is a blessing--
her conversation is addiction--
made it past infatuation this feeling is genuine--
her eyes out-jeweled the stars in splendor,
 I didn't lust for her but vowed to always remember--
every moment together is so tender-
I never say goodnight, just let her know I appreciate her in my life--
definite, one of a kind-
her mind, contains rare jewels that you can't find-
darling, you send me in a place of grace that will never be replaced--
every minute is a second, but every second is a lifetime-
offer my patience, she's the seed of inspiration for sincerity in a relationship--
it's heaven, it's meant for every being living--
it's a miracle how,
the world can revolve around an individual
when you escape the physical, and involve the spiritual--

DREAM GIRL 2

I could be,
influenced by dynasties empires kingdoms
n everything powerful that's fascinating fine women//
However I believe in a love from heaven
 that's equivalent to goddesses, beauty queens, fresh, ele-
gantly, flawlessly,
 takin my heart making it heavenly//
 honestly baby you astonish me //
diamonds, pearls, n gold, lady this world could be yours//
 take tours. Paris to Rome; Alaska, Hawaii n then back home /
/oh my you're so fly, the sky you must own/
/we're like the sun n the moon forever alone//
 however, just as important to every aspect of life/
/ with all due respect girl in time you'd create a perfect wife//
 be the day shine n be our children's light// I'll make the sacri-
fice n be the cold dark night/
/ I'll change the tides hoping you come back to sight// hurri-
canes tsunamis tornadoes baby I'll fight with all my might to
never let go my oh so special angel//
forever grateful, forever faithful, forever irreplaceable//
 simply a miracle, attracted physically but most definitely spiri-
tually//
 from a seed to a tree forever with me you shall be//
let our love blow in the wind be free// I don't need you and
you don't need me//
 but we're each-others other wing n we both have dreams

believing we could fly/

/so tell me why we keep wasting our time with other dimes or other guys//

betrayal of the hearts a pitiful crime, and the world's worst lie//

take it easy grab my heart slow dance //I'll sing in your ear, tell you "don't fear your king is right here" //

sweet romance every single day,

just need one chance, forget all our regrets never look back//

put all the drama away, happiness will stay,

fall asleep look in your eyes, tell you that I love you every single day we wake//

till the lord comes and one our souls he takes n makes,

the heart earthquake n break//

let's enjoy today cuz time is only borrowed!

Through all the pain n suffering, I give you thanks again my reason for tomorrow...

Easy to Be Hopeless

We asked for liberty, they gave us slavery.

They fight for oppression, it's bravery--

we fight for freedom, it's savagery--

On the reservation, birthing confused generations.

God said have patience, I'll be your salvation--

but I can't stand by and watch the suicide of my nation--

What is true grace?

I believe in our kids// to be better than us,

we'll survive I trust, I mean I must.

In this process it's

Easy to be hopeless, hard to be hopeful--

witnessing the genocide of native people around the world is

drowning my soul--

What's the point of caring anymore? This is a world of greed,

kill us all in the name of progress,

rape the indigenous enjoy the profit//

turned what's sacred, into their make-up--

mascot, mass graves, masses rot, masses forgot, massive lies

taught--

and If I speak up, I'm weak. What?--

I ain't holding my composure--

I'm exploding vultures, killing my culture--

making kids foreigners in their own land--

coroners examining a young dead man--

said it was the "coronas on the corners, straight to the head"

damn—

Faith

Most obsess possessions,
my lesson is material is evanescent
 real blessings is everlasting heaven sent
it doesn't evaporate my aim is to eliminate the hate the ideas
that lead to discriminate,
 multiple beliefs could exist there's no superior race
we don't need to look the same,
 they say that's an obstacle that's impossible
 why don't chu strive for something logical?
 Well, I evict a scientist's evidence, it's evident this confidence
is god's wish--
 his plan for me is well thought out, I grew up in the devils
house, grew close to demons--
 Faith kept me dreaming, now my spirit has woke, time to
evoke the solution for the revolution--
 evolved to solve the problems and dissolve the doubt--
 it's no longer a mystery--
 I will be posthumous in history--
 murk the misery this poem is the entry--
 two decades in, hopefully I'll survive to at least a quarter
century--
 If I don't let me be at peace, don't drown yourself in reminisc-
ing, cuz my struggles I sure as hell won't be missing--
I'm heaven sent, immaterial hero,
soon as they think I'm immanent, I break physics taking it to a
limit never seen before///

my words migrate out my mind, between the lines and
immerse in a verse, that should be illegal--
you get it?
I find moral in a world of immorality--
 inequality is reality--
flip words to last eternity, I survived my own savagery--
 hope they remember me, gift this knowledge immortality--
I'm immune to what ruins the mind of a reZervation kid--
 I guess that makes me dangerous, full of scars but no slit
wrists--
 a witness to what truly exists
depression, depression, depression, NOPE!! Not the economy
crashing--
Oppression! Oppression! Oppression!!!!

Honor Us

Honor your women--

young and dreaming--

stripped from home--

sitting in the boarding schools--

still full with soul--

abuse after abuse, still holding hope--

9 months, wombs cradling warriors--

mothers and sisters webbing the future--

nesting the next blessings--

 so, may your lover be your best friend --

out in the battlefield --

she kept our language alive--

she kept our songs alive--

she kept our dances alive--

telling her it's illegal--

washing her mouth out with soap --

beating her till she turned purple --

 just know, she fought for you--

she spoke to free you!

we can't forget that,

we're here because of her--

if there's a tomorrow we must honor her--

otherwise we might as well be the ones harming her--

thrown in a room locked and scared, she dared to dream--

brought us together--

cuz of her we'll be here forever--

I love you!

I'll go to war for you--

there's so much more for you--

I adore you--

I'm thankful --

Stay courageous, it's contagious!

Savior of the nations

thank you for being patient--

the love you injected in me can't be replaced, your bravery

saved an entire race!

and I can't wait to see the heavenly smile upon your face--

the day your sons come home again--

the things she endured in her life, I never wanna see in my

wife--

so I know being a man is much more than being a male and

I'm focusing on doing it right—

I Don't Understand

I don't understand a lot of things like,a diet soda-
drive thru pills and drive thru burgers
kill more than drive thru shooters--
glamorizing celebrities that don't contribute to society--
ignoring the real heroes--
"Wow Kim Kardashian wears a pink dress! Mandela pased away?
Who's that?"
the statue of liberty, when there's so many oppressed--
The deliberate dumbing down of the education systems--
Shutting down schools in the poor communities, then building
more prisons
Guess the place, those children are expected to live in--
hope in the little circumstances they can enchant it, enhance it,
and advance it-
the clarity of prosperity appears despairingly--
They teach you to fear men in the streets, that talk with a slang n
hang under hoodies-
They don't teach you about the white collar criminals that's in
offices, designing failures of our communities-
Who do you think blueprinted the projects?
Before brothers were drug smuggling, they were on slave ships
smuggled in--
Before Natives were addicted to an alcoholics binge, they were
stripped of everything that meant to them--
Before brothers were caught hustling rocks, on blocks; they were
sold on auction blocks--

speak like Malala --

Speak like Rumi

Geronimo-

Sitting Bull-

A Palestinian kid at an Israeli check point, pushed to the boiling point-

A child from Sudan-

A native Brazilian, willing to take a bullet from the corporations--

A refuge camped baby, patiently waiting for some food from the United Nations--

Unwarranted and unwanted, born haunted, fight back, stop it, Heaven is yours---

i vs. Eye

All these Adams and Eves are obsessed with the Apple--

"look at my iPhone, look at all iGot, iDon't care about helping

you or anybody, I'm out to get what iWant!"--

"iFlaunt miWatch, iBought the new iMac, what iDon't realize is

all that iLack"--

well eye respond with, "eyeCare, eyeShare, eyeLove, eyeLis-

ten"--

eyeAm not a follower,

eyeGot my own dreams, eyeGot my own visions, eyeSee

the divine reality, eyeBattle with my self cuz eyeSee nobody is

going to help--

they just deceive you…

When your consumerism addictions gets you in a prison, and

you're wondering where did iGo-wrong—eyeWill, show you

what to really strive for, eyeWill make you feel alive like never

before--

Once you learn to live happily without the fallacy dreams of a

magazine--

eyeDon't care about Facebook thumbs or Youtube views--

everybody wants to be famous, everybody is self-obsessive,

well I am not impressed with an attention addicts best wish--

I don't feed into it--

I am worried about our kids--

how are we going to raise a generation far better than society

ever did for us--

How can I be in love with me?

When I see people committing, the same exact thing they hate?

That's the non-dictionary description of poverty and slavery--
To repeat is the only way to escape. That's false though,
I know I am here to open eyes and give back hope--
 I don't need the praise of a man in a cape--
 I just need you to break these mirrors insecurities, and live with faith-

just live with faith, that's all I need is YOU to live with faith!!

Misery of History

We must begin with the misrepresentation and transform it into what is true. That is, we must uncover the source of the misrepresentation, otherwise, hearing what is true won't help us. The truth cannot penetrate when something is taking its place.

Genocide does not necessarily mean the immediate destruction of a nation, except when accomplished by mass killing.. It is intended rather to signify a coordinated plan of different actions aiming at the destruction of the essential foundations of the life of national groups, with the aim of annihilating the groups themselves.

Genocide itself is defined in a two-fold way, encompassing all policies intended to precipitate 1. The destruction of such a group 2. Preventing its preservation and development.

If a people suddenly lose their "prime symbol", the basis of culture, their lives lose meaning. Become disorientated, with no hope. As social disorganization often follows such loss, they are often unable to ensure their own survival…The loss and human suffering for those whose culture has been healthy and is suddenly attacked and disintegrated are incalculable.

It's illegal to use my language they don't want us to speak--
illegal to hunt whale they don't want us to eat--
throw us alcohol to drink, they want us to lose our ability to

think--

Wise word from Technique "though we survived through the struggles that made us

we look at ourselves through the eyes of the people that hate us"--

meaning we believe we're failures--

the drug problem is proof a lot of us gave up--

but I could be your voice young warrior wake up--

we could impact the world--

we survived measles, mumps, small pox--

my people so strong we can take on an atomic bomb!

Nothing but love exists in heart don't get me wrong--

but the Makah come from the bravest--

no matter the dangers, our ancestors saved us--

there's tribes who don't know who they are

and some even extinct--

fighting through residential schools--

Fighting cultural assimilation--

fighting separation of my nation

throughout the generations--

fighting institutionalized racism--

fighting self-hatred--

surviving the reservation

prison system--

they found a way for preservation--

I'm thankful for our gift from the past--

how long will it last?

We're in the cycle of genocide, where they can stand back

and say look what they're doing to themselves--

Remember the struggle, teach our truth--
please keep killing me Miss America because I am far from
civilized,
Boarding schools still exist, and we cannot pass classes unless
we write about your lies of history--
our answers are correct, but if we write them down you'll look
at us and tell us we have no respect--
if we don't sing the national anthem or salute the flag, you'll
say I'm a disgrace and I should move from this place--
we're from this place, disgraced and placed in a mass grave--
So thank you to the unknown heroes of the past, that'll never
be spoken of--
that'd illegally speak their language, that would illegally say
their prayers--
that'd illegally sing their songs, that'd illegally teach our truth.--
We must change the way we live, treat each-other better n
get back to our roots--

Life's Unpredictab

my ambition has me higher than th

I'm patient but it's not time to be sl

you lose your youth so your mind r

my heart was pure, black, now pul

/thankful I'm here,

don't chu know when I speak I glow//

/ to the unknown I go /far from this atmosphere, with no fear to show//

//because that's somethin I never owned// in the army of god I was made/

/ so in front of mortal man why should I be afraid//

fight sin/

no metal bullet could penetrate my skin//

my weapon's my brain n when I pull, it's firing truth to deception// to heal n offer protection //

got kicked out of school, I never liked mathematics

//the promise of what's to equal is broken//

from me let truth always be spoken//

they treated me like I was eligible for lethal injection//

I stood up for the plan was to make me hate my own reflection//

expelled for speaking my language, institutional racism existed /

/they'd take facts from the past n twist em in sick visions//

I'm not afraid cuz I know I'm meant to be one of those who struggle for the heavenly//

immortality will be m

whom the creator

//So I walk car

that's cryin

In my

ev

reality //magically turning savagery to

made us set out to be//

lessly through Riots n violence// N the sirens

g// The lyin starts dyin, the truth turnin to triumph//

rain I contain ways to remain through the pain //lost

rything, being able to breathe means you have everything

to gain// walkin ,soakin in the rain livin against the grain// cloak-

ing the side of me that's insane// prides chocking can't let him

break from his chains //Lava rushing through my veins, trying to

kill my warrior ways// people like me just don't exist these days

//surrounded by cowards with no will power/ it frustrates they

scared to say, they scared to receive hate// they would rath-

er have love that's fake, than stand up n be the voice of the

forgotten race! //Why the hell should I change I'll be the same

till maggots is eating the skin off my face.

Martin Luther King Kong

I'm never afraid to stand alone In my beliefs because//
If I could travel between the past and the future //
I bet if I go back and warn Martin Luther //
if you speak today they'll shoot cha//
he'll still stand up in the podium// speaking dreams of free-
dom//
knowing he's saying his last words of wisdom//
Yes! I got the same courage as him// so my heart I leak when I
speak n that don't make me weak,
 it's just that// Don't chu know you kill your own soul /when you
pick up the bottle and foil//
watch the pill burn slow n the liquor flow/emotions, you're losin
control//
 making black marks your spirits turnin dark//
 take a breath, another spark, another shot, another scar//
we're constantly killin ourselves and never learning//
what's it all earnin? We could be extinct and the world will keep
turnin? //
So here is the sermon please continue your genocide //
cuz I still ain't civilized//
I'm only speaking peacefully for mankind //
you ever stare into a child's eyes n wanna cry //
cuz that innocence is goin to die, mothers and fathers would
rather get high //
it's a shame but the addicts ain't the ones to blame //

alot of us quit prayin, the same days we stopped playin//

don't be judgmental is what I'm sayin //

I'm not just gon be another victim slain, not goin to drown in my pain, fearless hearts pumpin blood to my veins //

step up, help out do all what God's about//

I'm a strong presence, fighting for the adolescents//

who's in danger of life sentences of depression //lackin lessons of blessins,

beautiful essence, since sin convinced, men to forsake him//

y'all getting it mistaken I was in need of saving//

been forgiven, livin in the grave// barely breathing, addicted to thoughts of leaving//

now my testimony gives even heathens something to believe in//

I'm kind of intergalactic how I opposite their tactics, magic how I didn't drown in all the tragic// //indeed I exceed what they call limits, never timid//

The pills everyone is smokin now was already a well-known power of addiction//

before the doctors even made the prescriptions //

now listen to the vision I'll claim sobriety for everyone// if they take credit for all the convictions//

it's sickening let's take a look to the beginning//

They taught you to fear Savages then, Kamikazes and Nazis//

now it's fear terrorists with bombs on a vest//

we still have blood on our palms from the napalms, and atom bombs// remote control drones//

the small pox blankets in every aboriginals home still ain't

gone//

I could tell cuz I was born with a soul torn//

I'm an individualist, a solitary man, penitentiary penitent //

alone is what I like to be ,but a true home is what I'd love to see//

My anger is indomitable that's why I dream the impossible//

I have faith that's stronger than anything logical, unstoppable//

my defense is impregnable, I create the unimaginable //

introduce you to my mind and I'll induce yours, impregnate it and breed new thought//

scars of inequality is crawling in me //

there's no other person I'd rather be, what others cry about I smile happily//

I'm glad to be a minority/ however I must say I'm wiser than the majority/

I live under one authority/ that represents righteousness, and honesty/

honestly I'm comfortable in hostility// I got the ability to define reality//

I'm divine In these new times riding high, a deity n forgiveness is real let me take you with me//

they tried to make me emotionless, but I never let go of my dreams through any tribulation//

So here I am like Martin Luther King//

looking at the crowd like a mirror, seeing my vision clearer

not asking will they shootchya? But, go out there n do what I sposta...

WARNING

My rhyme patterns is ridiculous-

time shatters when I'm kickin it -

pieces flying, slow motion frames-

reflecting hopes of change--

projectin emotions of rage--

ejecting words to the page--

your injecting the verses I made--

respecting the art I create--

even if it's a subject you hate--

I gotchu biting the bait n, you can't wait till the next line-

you start to feel anxious like a predator biting your neck--

now take a deep breeaaathhee

ahhhh--

they call that addiction--

I could hear you loud as you listen in silence--

playing with your mind, convicting your thoughts to violence--

trying to comprehend it

you're going to have a hard time--

making amends with what I really meant--

Penmanship that sinks ships, brainwave tsunamis--

nothing on me, drowning armies--

armed with thoughts--

if you're lost

map the lines out--

we could have the same view but, it's hard to see what I see--

cuz I be seas apart, floatin on a different cloud-

Open with caution, don't get caught in the dark...

Merry Go Round

Sometimes I wonder why, I feel like the
"Y" in eye--
then I realize why, I see the world differently--
Sometimes eye is capitalized, and the other e feels greater
than thee on the other side--
never understood why, but being the Y made me see both of
them--
they are the same,
I don't fit with either--
I'm with them but surrounded by myself--
they look at me strange like, "why, Y are you different than I?--"
I explain, upper class or lower class, I'm just a class act--
however, not nothing like an act, just all fact like Snapple
cap--
got millions lying for millions--
I'm the lion in the million--
the ion on the lion--
not lying, millions would want to be part of the heart of the lion
but they're lying
Building empires from debris, from the empires in debris
I inspire empires that will not debris or fall to the seas
self-consciousness brain waves tsunami the seas, tsunami
society...

Tears of a Flower

Tears dropping from a flower
 makes her grow from the lies of a coward--
it falls into the soils of her soul,
 devours her self-respect for wrapping her roots into a fool--
she smiles bright colors on the top--
 the stems is her heart
 n they're the same color--
 nobody notices who approaches,
 it's like she walks her emotions in the realms of ghosts--
 I just hope she could cope--
 for she has power of pollen--
which we all rely on--
 attached to the earth--
 n could develop birth
to even the fool who makes her hurt--
it's a Shame the majority don't understand the values she's
worth!

Shakespeare

I dream of changes/
up in these classes, they treat me like I can't pass and it's frus-
trating/
maybe it's cuz I talk with a slang/
speak undefined words like conversate instead of converse//
they think that I can't hang/
looking at me like I'm illiterate, if I spoke my vocabulary geek's
wouldn't get it/
You'd have to go to Harvard to divide it, conquer it, and com-
prehend it/
I just don't care about wasting breath articulating a coherent
sentence for your acceptance.
My art is stimulating, it's apparent you can't bare it, I'm a prodi-
gy not an apprentice, no exceptions//
IF Shakespeare were here he'd revere, standing in fear feeling
severe// it'd be like looking in a mirror
however I'm on top of the pyramid, point blank period/
word play is myriad,
no scientific entities, just spirit//
I kept this simplistic, so you don't have to Google the words I
mentioned//

Did he just elevate himself above Shakespeare?

Na, you better keep it together like a joint/
I'm just proving a point//

Scares Hidden

To judge by outer detail is frail n will fail--

most don't see souls so I close my eyes n sail through my
dreams//

connecting to different galaxies, complexities appearing
simply--

split personalities make me learn quickly--

the downside though is the same thing that I love hurts me,

the same I love hurts me, what hurts me I love, why? `

I question why, look up in the sky, see one figure holding my

heart n see numerous ones holding the broken side--

God is here, something in me loves these devils inside--

Soon as I get the first opportunity to escape I will--

see my people killing ourselves everyday off the alcohol n

pills--

I wish I could tell y'all it's a movie, but it's real....

lemme show you how genocide feels don't get addicted to

the thrill--

Sounds entertaining looking into our lives, this pain n sinning is

never ending

man I ain't pretending...

Lemme take you to the beginning--

Young bucks down on they luck, drinking in smoking before

the age of thirteen--

where in the world did life get so mean?--

we used to be running around playing, now pay attention to

what I'm saying--

last night there was partying n wilding, come home from school flirting with the girls smiling-- enter the room, his mom-mas eye's black n blue--

the violence is constant man, why she sticking with this fool?-- swear when he's bigger he going to pay him back, frustrated as hell no time to relax--

Oh no, they on a binge, sneak out the window go stay at your best friends--

Next morning same thing again, all the adults past out, see the drugs in the syringe?--

He's starving, no food in the cabinet--

starts to steal n that becomes a bad habit--

so now he's stealing, got the feeling it's easy, thinking he made a big score--

gave money to his older homies, to get as much from the liquor store--

drank until he was poor--

It's surprising he went through that without realizing, he was doing the same thing, he's tryna hide from..

Life goes by, now he has a son,

who with... who with? The girl he used to love now he only refers to her as a bitch!

He was just innocent--

stuck in the past, looking past his son, doesn't care about buy-ing diapers he'd rather get high--

Now watch the cycle begin!

I hope he escape though, I hope he escape though, find someone beautiful n be faithful, work hard, so the innocent won't turn fatal…scars hidden…

Posthumous

I used to have suicidal thoughts now heaven is my home
 Now, here's some thoughts that roamed into my zone.......
 I'm a hypocritical political criminal, it's despicable--
 I'll shake hands with rapists, I'll laugh at the victim as long as
the guilty ones money exists locked in my   fists//
I'm a judge with a gavel locking up the innocent for the color
of their skin--
how else we going compete with cheap labor?
you're now government owned you're a legal slave sir--
I'm a banker denying loans I know you could payback but
accepting, the ones I know you won't so I could possess your
home and everything you own//
 it's the legal way to put a gun to your dome, comply or die!!//
Let the truth be shown!!
 I'm a doctor prescribing medicine of addiction
you're a patient you ain't no victim
 I'm killing your brain cells welcome to hell, this is a hustle don't
listen to a nutritionist//
 pay your intuition I'm a teacher I'll show you what
an education is, better listen or die damn savages//
don't be a fool
this isn't a boarding school/ now listen to everything I say,
pledge allegiance to this murderous flag--
forget everything you know, praise the Heroes that discovered
this beautiful home...
Columbus, George Washington, Abraham Lincoln, you know

all the good men, that called my fathers heathens--
I'm Obama ordering remote control drones//
 I'm President Bush reading a book while the towers are getting blown!
 I'm the lynch mob raping then hanging a black woman for showing emotion!
I'm the cavalry leaders shaking hands with the indigenous, giving em gifts of small pox!
 I'm the man who dropped the atomic bomb! I'm the man who shot Martin Luther King cuz he was wrong! Peace isn't real the blind can't understand how I feel,
 such a beautiful place to live but you are only free if you're willing to be a slave//
 I'm the officer who shot John T Williams and got away, I'm the devil in evil men I'm here to stay/
I'm the men who slaughtered native children and scalped their heads for some bread//
 I hate how people say look how strong you came along, like my people's history started with misery,
like alcoholism existed, like cursing existed, we had wars but not borders we fought for what we believed not following a greedy man's orders//
 they talk about my society, I hated school, couldn't stand in silence while teachers lied to me//
 came here to civilize us but, who taught us the opposite of trust? Who taught us drugs? Who taught poor kids to wanna be thugs, and bust slugs for a pocket full of change?
It's strange, forget Benjamin Franklin why would I thank him or wanna possess him? When

I represent the souls starving and rotten in the slave ships, fighting against cowards with whips// I'm the peaceful man that used to exist, now considered a savage, a labeled terrorist, I got blood shot eyes of war, with no forgiveness//

Panopticon Nation

Mind entombed in a womb of unceremonious catacombs--
Twists and turns that never learn--
running out of oxygen trying to get out of sight of this
panopticon--
slaved, pushed down under by the man in the rotunda--
if faith gave a flicker of a candle, turn it into lightning
and burn overseers--
storms free us-
let the mute speak thunder-
acidic lines to erode the cages-
blood spilled on pages
raged with a road to redemption-
bust out of prison no dead end-
cuz the condition we live in; will leave us dead, no happy
end--
My mind was entombed in a womb of unceremonious
catacombs-
enslaved to the unknown-
foreign in my own home-
born in this war zone-
will the sky ever be seen again?-
will we ever be free, will we ever be who we are meant to be?-

Tears

Baby girl eight years old -
stolen from her mother-
even though no-one cares, this poem is for her tears…
the first few nights her price was high-
she'd cry, she'd cry, she'd cry-
trying to hide under her covers that wouldn't comfort her-
reaching out for a hand to grab searching for her mothers..
She's confused, the pain never felt like this before--
she's thinking "you look exactly like my dad but I was never hurt
by him before."-
"Who are you?" The pain stopped, "wait where are you going?"
now another man is walking in--
eventually, every visit is much cheaper--
her souls so torn, she's not even crying no more--
She's not even asking why no more--
moved her from the specialty to the discount store--
on the menu for sinister men like a restaurant in hell--
she's there now because she's considered used up, too
drugged up--
they don't buy her clothes no more, they took all her posses-
sions n gave em to the new one--
stripping an innocent heart, where's humanity? it's insanity--
she don't even remember what her name used to be --
she only responds to a number, dreams don't exist when she's
deep in her slumber--
only nightmares, but she's so used to it she don't care --

the older she gets the less she even tries, --

she actually does have every right in life to make suicide

seem right..

average of ten a day --

I'm not even going to call them men, I don't even know what I

should say to replace that phrase--

However she don't even mind to store in mind their faces,

she is the victim of so many exchanges--

not too long ago she was a diamond always smiling, the most

important soul of her whole family--

I cannot imagine this insanity, I hope you gain the courage to

flee--

Hop up out that window and never stop running--

I have no clue how, I pray you discover the sun again--

I pray you feel safe under-covers again --

I pray you never forget nor, never just settle and live with it--

but forgive yourself, and treat yourself

like the diamond you are--

try to learn to love again --

respect yourself, find a real man to love you, hold you, mold

you to the woman you're supposed to be--

every-day he better treat you respectfully --

then hopefully you breathe happily..

All the faces you saw are not men and, while you are residing

in the stars

they will be in slavery for eternity--

and baby,

you shall be free……….

Place of Replacement

Rain splatters the window of a dark room--

soft voice trembling, talking about life back then--

as tears roll down to the floor, an elder telling me that there is

nothing sacred no more--

so I chose to fight evil as my thing to live for--

To all of our children born in this war--

May your death be as beautiful as your birth--

may your every breath bring worth--

May your dreams fly like the birds--

n lay your dirt with the worms--

are you dreaming what I' believe in?

Fiend for freedom' are you seeing what I'm seeing?

Too many leaders deceiving--

not enough people caring--

our kids have thoughts of leaving, before their baby teeth fill

in--

it wears and tears--

we all know whose responsible for these killings--

but we're cowards so we whisper--

we're cowards so we whisper--

we're cowards so we whisper--

the end could be near,

so I hope you hear me clear--

stand without fear, change is here-

Feel it in the air--

devils beware--

spare the despair--

I wish I could explain how much I care--

but hearing these stories of these anomalies that came with
no apologies--

I only offer back a blank stare--

wishing I had the power to repair, what was once there--

n yeah, the circumstances could be unfair-

but remember we come from a bloodline of warriors
that'd storm a shore--

then ask the enemy " Why are you crying now, you're the one
who challenged me"--

so I sprint into the thick of the mess, send me your best--

I'm sick of the stress, won't you show me the correct steps--

when I'm laid to rest, allow me to wake with the most blessed--

remind the world,

I was equipped with the;

spirit of a wolf, instincts of a tiger, and the same heart that
pumps in a lion's chest-